SO-AVQ-936

Renditions of Tahoe

Juan Acosta,
Beata & Eric Jarvis

Sunset on south shore ~ Eric

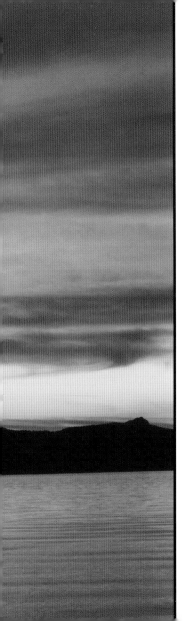

Foreword

Lake Tahoe is truly one of nature's gems. Because of its many facets and its natural splendor, it captivates the photographer's eye.

This book is an effort to present some aspects of the Lake that we find most compelling. Due to its beauty and grandeur, we constantly discover new sights and details in Tahoe's ever-changing landscape.

The "Renditions of Tahoe" project was a year in the making. During this time we went out for many cold sunrises and strenuous hikes which were rewarding beyond description. We feel fortunate to be able to enjoy the serenity of the area in which we live and work.

We hope you like what you find here.

For additional breathtaking images of Lake Tahoe and several other exotic locations, please visit our online galleries.

www.jarvisgallery.com
&
www.vistapanorama.com

Echo Falls
~ Eric

Eagle Falls ~ Eric

Echo Falls ~ Juan

Lavender dawn ~ Eric

Kayaker at Secret Cove ~ Juan

Frozen shore ~ Juan

Snowy curves ~ Juan

Winter sunrise over Mt. Tallac ~ Eric

A close look at a dandelion ~ Beata

Adolescent black bear ~ Eric

Rocky bottom of Lake Tahoe's east shore ~ Eric

Tranquil waters of Tahoe at the Thunderbird Lodge ~ Juan

Sunset at Bonsai Rock ~ Juan

Fannette Island
at Emerald Bay
~ Eric

Fractured ice at
Emerald Bay
~ Juan

Butterflies ~ Eric

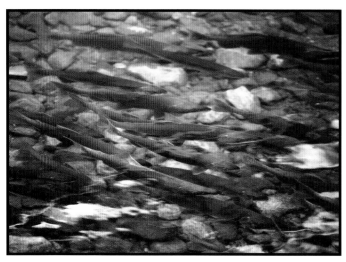

Salmon run at Taylor Creek ~ Beata

Coyote ~ |Eric

Striking morning light on Mt. Tallac ~ Juan

Sunny side up ~ Juan

Autumn leaves ~ Juan

Snow plant ~ Juan

Sunset from Edgewood pier ~ Eric

Spring blossoms at Cathedral Meadow ~ Eric

Frozen trees at the Tahoe Keys ~ Juan

Serene sunrise, Emerald Bay
~ Juan

Tahoe pebbles ~ Eric

Rocks in calm water, east shore ~ Eric

Wispy clouds over Mt. Tallac ~ Eric

Autumn blaze ~ Eric

Autumn leaves flowing in Carson River ~ Eric

Red berries ~ Juan

Eagle Falls in the early morning sun ~ Juan

Morning dew ~ Eric

Delicate fern ~ Eric

Sunrise mist ~ Juan

Floating leaf ~ Juan

Fall colors in Hope Valley
~ Juan

Summer sunset, Edgewood ~ Juan

Blue sky over aspen trees
~ Beata

Changing fall colors ~ Eric

Autumn foliage at Spooner Summit ~ Eric

Moss on sequoia ~ Juan

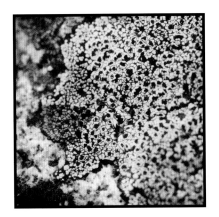

Lichen on the rocks
~ Juan

Moss covered rock, Echo Summit ~ Juan

Zephyr Cove sunset ~ Eric

Bear-clawed aspens ~ Eric

Wildflowers atop Mt. Tallac ~ Juan

Mt. Tallac from Zephyr Heights ~ Juan

Zephyr Cove sunset ~ Juan

Sunrise bird, Emerald Bay ~ Eric

Luminance ~ Eric

Lenticular clouds over Lake Tahoe ~ Juan

Reflection of Mt. Tallac over Fallen Leaf Lake ~ Beata

Eagle Falls ~ Eric

Mt. Tallac in the morning sun ~ Eric

Snowy branch
~ Eric

Tahoe sunset from Cave Rock ~ Juan

Geese flying over Edgewood ~ Eric

Aspen leaves in the wind ~ Juan

Wildflowers of Glenbrook ~ Eric

Fiery sunset on the south shore ~ Juan

Juan Acosta

A native of Colombia, South America, Juan moved to the United States with his mother in 1996.

Since 1998 his unique vision and passion for photography have motivated him to explore the medium. He began his career as a portrait and event photographer, operating his own studio in Huntsville, Alabama, where he also worked with his great friend, photographer David Phillips.

In 2003, upon moving to Lake Tahoe, the stunning vistas of the High Sierra inspired his shift into scenic photography. Juan has traveled with Eric throughout the American West documenting its endless beauty.

He currently runs his fine art photography gallery at www.vistapanorama.com.

Eric and Juan working on the next book
~ Photo by self timer

Beata & Eric Jarvis

Beata and Eric Jarvis are professional photographers based in Stateline, Nevada near the shores of beautiful Lake Tahoe.

Their photography pursuits have taken them to many exotic places including Vietnam, Cambodia, Bora Bora, Bulgaria, Croatia, Turkey and Russia.

Of all the remarkable locations that they have been fortunate enough to capture in their images, Lake Tahoe remains the most fascinating.

"Lake Tahoe is, of course, one of nature's great treasures. It is also an amazing resource for the scenic photographer; there is always something new, a different aspect of the lake's beauty to explore. The snow-capped peaks, the play of the water and rocks, the many ways of a Tahoe sunrise... I am thankful to be able to live and work in such a breathtaking place."
- Eric Jarvis

View more of their work at their online gallery at www.jarvisgallery.com.

© 2007 Juan Acosta, Beata & Eric Jarvis

All rights reserved. No portion of this book may be reproduced or utilized in any form, without the prior written permission of the publishers.

Juan Acosta
Vista Panorama
P.O. Box 11696
Zephyr Cove, NV 89448
info@vistapanorama.com
(888) 667-3575

Beata & Eric Jarvis
Jarvis Gallery
P.O. Box 7194
Stateline, NV 89449
images@jarvisgallery.com
(800) 452-7864

Printed in Colombia by
Panamericana Formas e Impresos S.A.

Print coordination in Colombia by
Pagina Maestra Editores
info@paginamaestra.com

ISBN 978-1-4243-3776-7

Ducks at Kiva Beach ~ Eric